LOVE POEMS

PIATKUS

© 1984 Judy Piatkus (Publishers) Limited

First published in 1984 by Judy Piatkus
(Publishers) Limited, London

Designed by Ken Leeder

Typeset by Phoenix Photosetting, Chatham
Printed and bound by The Pitman Press, Bath

ISBN 0–86188–424–8

CONTENTS

5 MEETING . . .

19 MATING . . .

29 LIVING TOGETHER . . .

43 PARTING . . .

62 INDEX OF POETS AND POEMS

64 ACKNOWLEDGEMENTS

MEETING ♥ ♥ ♥

CHRISTINA ROSSETTI
THE FIRST DAY

I wish I could remember the first day,
First hour, first moment of your meeting me;
If bright or dim the season, it might be
Summer or winter for aught I can say.
So unrecorded did it slip away,
So blind was I to see and to foresee,
So dull to mark the budding of my tree
That would not blossom yet for many a May.

If only I could recollect it! Such
A day of days! I let it come and go
As traceless as a thaw of bygone snow.
It seemed to mean so little, meant so much!
If only now I could recall that touch,
First touch of hand in hand! – Did one but know!

♥ ♥ ♥

RUPERT BROOKE
THE HILL

Breathless, we flung us on the windy hill,
Laughed in the sun, and kissed the lovely grass.
You said, 'Through glory and ecstasy we pass;
Wind, sun, and earth remain, the birds sing still,
When we are old, are old. . . .' 'And when we die
All's over that is ours; and life burns on
Through other lovers, other lips,' said I,
'Heart of my heart, our heaven is now, is won!'

'We are Earth's best, that learnt her lesson here.
Life is our cry. We have kept the faith!' we said;
'We shall go down with unreluctant tread
Rose-crowned into the darkness! '. . . Proud we were,
And laughed, that had such brave true things to say.
– And then you suddenly cried, and turned away.

ANON

FOURTH CENTURY

PLUCKING THE RUSHES

A boy and a girl are sent to gather rushes for thatching

Green rushes with red shoots,
Long leaves bending to the wind –
You and I in the same boat
Plucking rushes at the Five Lakes.

We started at dawn from the orchid-island:
We rested under elms till noon.
You and I plucking rushes
Had not plucked a handful when night came!

Translated from the Chinese by
Arthur Waley

ISAAC ROSENBERG
<u>YOU AND I</u>

You and I have met but for an instant;
And no word the gate-lips let from out them.
But the eyes, voice audible – the soul's lips,
Stirr'd the depths of thought and feeling in me.

I have seen you somewhere, some sweet sometime,
Somewhere in a dim-remembered sometime.
Was it in the sleep-spun realm of dreamland?
In sweet woods, a faery flower of fancy?

If our hands touched would it bring us nearer?
As our souls touched, eyes' flame meeting eyes' flame.
If the lips spake would it lift the curtain
More than our mute bearing unaffected
Told the spirit's secrets eloquently?

Strange! this vast and universal riddle!
How perplexing! Manifold the wonder.
You and I, we meet but for an instant,
Pause or pass, reflections in a mirror.
And I see myself and wonder at it.
See myself in you, a double wonder.
With my thought held in a richer casket,
Clothed and girt in shape of regal beauty.
Strange! we pause! New waves of life rush blindly,
Madly on the soul's dumb silent breakers.

And a music strange is new awakened.
Fate the minstrel smites or holds the chord back.
Smites – new worlds undreamt of burst upon us.
All our life before was but embryo
Shaping for this birth – this living moment.

H. BELLOC
<u>JULIET</u>

How did the party go in Portman Square?
I cannot tell you; Juliet was not there.
And how did Lady Gaster's party go?
Juliet was next me and I do not know.

SIR JOHN BETJEMAN
A SUBALTERN'S LOVE-SONG

Miss J. Hunter Dunn, Miss J. Hunter Dunn,
Furnish'd and burnish'd by Aldershot sun,
What strenuous singles we played after tea,
We in the tournament – you against me!

Love-thirty, love-forty, oh! weakness of joy,
The speed of a swallow, the grace of a boy,
With carefullest carelessness, gaily you won,
I am weak from your loveliness, Joan Hunter Dunn.

Miss Joan Hunter Dunn, Miss Joan Hunter Dunn,
How mad I am, sad I am, glad that you won.
The warm-handled racket is back in its press,
But my shock-headed victor, she loves me no less.

Her father's euonymus shines as we walk,
And swing past the summer-house, buried in talk,
And cool the verandah that welcomes us in
To the six-o'clock news and a lime-juice and gin.

The scent of the conifers, sound of the bath,
The view from my bedroom of moss-dappled path,
As I struggle with double-end evening tie,
For we dance at the Golf Club, my victor and I.

On the floor of her bedroom lie blazer and shorts
And the cream-coloured walls are be-trophied with
sports,
And westering, questioning settles the sun
On your low-leaded window, Miss Joan Hunter Dunn.

The Hillman is waiting, the light's in the hall,
The pictures of Egypt are bright on the wall,
My sweet, I am standing beside the oak stair
And there on the landing's the light on your hair.

By roads 'not adopted', by woodlanded ways,
She drove to the club in the late summer haze,
Into nine-o'clock Camberley, heavy with bells
And mushroomy, pine-woody, evergreen smells.

Miss Joan Hunter Dunn, Miss Joan Hunter Dunn,
I can hear from the car-park the dance has begun.
Oh! full Surrey twilight! importunate band!
Oh! strongly adorable tennis-girl's hand!

Around us are Rovers and Austins afar,
Above us, the intimate roof of the car,
And here on my right is the girl of my choice,
With the tilt of her nose and the chime of her voice,

And the scent of her wrap, and the words never said,
And the ominous, ominous dancing ahead.
We sat in the car park till twenty to one
And now I'm engaged to Miss Joan Hunter Dunn.

JOHN BERRYMAN
FILLING HER COMPACT & DELICIOUS BODY

Filling her compact & delicious body
with chicken paprika, she glanced at me
twice.
Fainting with interest, I hungered back
and only the fact of her husband & four other people
kept me from springing on her

or falling at her little feet and crying
'You are the hottest one for years of night
Henry's dazed eyes
have enjoyed, Brilliance.' I advanced upon
(despairing) my spumoni.– Sir Bones: is stuffed,
de world, wif feeding girls.

– Black hair, complexion Latin, jewelled eyes
downcast . . . The slob beside her feasts . . . What
wonders is she sitting on, over there?
The restaurant buzzes. She might as well be on Mars.
Where did it all go wrong? There ought to be a law
    against Henry.
– Mr Bones: there is.

D. H. LAWRENCE
GLOIRE DE DIJON

When she rises in the morning
I linger to watch her;
She spreads the bath-cloth underneath the window
And the sunbeams catch her
Glistening white on the shoulders,
While down her sides the mellow
Golden shadow glows as
She stoops to the sponge, and her swung breasts
Sway like full-blown yellow
Gloire de Dijon roses.

She drips herself with water, and her shoulders
Glisten as silver, they crumple up
Like wet and falling roses, and I listen
For the sluicing of their rain-dishevelled petals.
In the window full of sunlight
Concentrates her golden shadow
Fold on fold, until it glows as
Mellow as the glory roses.

♥ ♥ ♥

ROBERT GRAVES
SYMPTOMS OF LOVE

Love is a universal migraine,
A bright stain on the vision
Blotting out reason.

Symptoms of true love
Are leanness, jealousy,
Laggard dawns;

Are omens and nightmares –
Listening for a knock,
Waiting for a sign:

For a touch of her fingers
In a darkened room,
For a searching look.

Take courage, lover!
Can you endure such grief
At any hand but hers?

DOROTHY PARKER
ONE PERFECT ROSE

A single flow'r he sent me, since we met.
    All tenderly his messenger he chose;
Deep-hearted, pure, with scented dew still wet –
    One perfect rose.

I knew the language of the floweret;
    'My fragile leaves', it said, 'his heart enclose'.
Love long has taken for his amulet
    One perfect rose.

Why is it no one ever sent me yet
    One perfect limousine, do you suppose?
Ah no, it's always just my luck to get
    One perfect rose.

MATING ♥ ♥ ♥

D. H. LAWRENCE
NEW YEAR'S EVE

There are only two things now,
The great black night scooped out
And this fireglow.

This fireglow, the core,
And we the two ripe pips
That are held in store.

Listen, the darkness rings
As it circulates round our fire.
Take off your things.

Your shoulders, your bruised throat!
Your breasts, your nakedness!
This fiery coat!

As the darkness flickers and dips,
As the firelight falls and leaps
From your feet to your lips!

E.E. CUMMINGS

---

i like my body when it is with your
body. It is so quite new a thing.
Muscles better and nerves more.
i like your body. i like what it does,
 i like its hows. i like to feel the spine
of your body and its bones, and the trembling
– firm-smooth ness and which i will
again and again and again
kiss, i like kissing this and that of you,
i like, slowly stroking the, shocking fuzz
of your electric fur, and what-is-it comes
over parting flesh . . . . And eyes big love-crumbs,

and possibly i like the thrill

of under me you so quite new

BRIAN PATTEN
<u>PARTY PIECE</u>

He said:

'Let's stay here
Now this place has emptied
And make gentle pornography with one another,
While the partygoers go out
And the dawn creeps in,
Like a stranger.

Let us not hesitate
Over what we know
Or over how cold this place has become,
But lets unclip our minds
And let tumble free
The mad, mangled crocodile of love.'

So they did,
There among the woodbines and guinness stains,
And later he caught a bus and she a train
And all there was between them then
was rain.

C. P. CAVAFY
TO REMAIN

It must have been one or one-thirty
after midnight.
        In a corner of the wine-shop;
behind the wooden partition.
Except for the two of us, the shop was completely
   deserted.
An oil lamp scarcely burning.
The waiter who had been awake,
slept now at the door.

No one would see us. But
we were so excited anyway
we couldn't take precautions.

We partly undid our clothes – there weren't many
as it was in divine burning July.

Enjoyment of flesh through
half-torn clothes;

quickly bared flesh; apparition
twenty-six years passed; and now returned
to remain in this poetry.

*Translated from the Greek by
Nikos Stangos and Stephen Spender*

PETRONIUS ARBITER

Good God, what a night that was,
The bed was so soft, and how we clung,
Burning together, lying this way and that,
Our uncontrollable passions
Flowing through our mouths.
If I could only die that way,
I'd say goodbye to the business of living

Translated from the Greek by
Kenneth Rexroth

YEHUDA AMICHAI
WE DID IT

We did it in front of the mirror
And in the light. We did it in darkness,
In water, and in the high grass.

We did it in honour of man
And in honour of beast and in honour of God.
But they didn't want to know about us,
They'd already seen our sort.

We did it with imagination and colours,
With confusion of reddish hair and brown
And with difficult gladdening
Exercises. We did it

Like wheels and holy creatures
And with chariot-feats of prophets.
We did it six wings
And six legs
        But the heavens
Were hard above us
Like the earth of the summer beneath.

Translated from the Hebrew by
Harold Schimmel

STEPHEN SPENDER
DAYBREAK

At dawn she lay with her profile at that angle
Which, when she sleeps, seems the carved face
                                        of an angel.
Her hair a harp, the hand of a breeze follows
And plays, against the white cloud of the pillows.
Then, in a flush of rose, she woke, and her eyes that
                                        opened
Swam in blue through her rose flesh that dawned.
From her dew of lips, the drop of one word
Fell like the first of fountains: murmured
'Darling', upon my ears the song of the first bird.
'My dream becomes my dream,' she said, 'come true.
I waken from you to my dream of you.'
Oh, my own wakened dream then dared assume
The audacity of her sleep. Our dreams
Poured into each other's arms, like streams.

♥ ♥ ♥

LIVING TOGETHER ♥ ♥ ♥

DOUGLAS DUNN
MODERN LOVE

It is summer, and we are in a house
That is not ours, sitting at a table
Enjoying minutes of a rented silence,
The upstairs people gone. The pigeons lull
To sleep the under-tens and invalids,
The tree shakes out its shadows to the grass,
The roses rove through the wilds of my neglect.
Our lives flap, and we have no hope of better
Happiness than this, not much to show for love
But how we are, or how this evening is,
Unpeopled, silent, and where we are alive
In a domestic love, seemingly alone,
All other lives worn down to trees and sunlight,
Looking forward to a visit from the cat.

HUGO WILLIAMS
TIDES

The evening advances, then withdraws again
Leaving our cups and books like islands on the floor.
We are drifting you and I,
As far from one another as the young heroes
Of these two novels we have just laid down.
For that is happiness: to wander alone
Surrounded by the same moon, whose tides remind us
   of ourselves,
Our distances, and what we leave behind.
The lamp left on, the curtains letting in the light.
These things were promises. No doubt we will come
   back to them.

ANNE STEVENSON
THE MARRIAGE

They will fit, she thinks,
but only if her backbone
cuts exactly into his rib cage,
and only if his knees
dock exactly under her knees
and all four
agree on a common angle.

All would be well
if only
they could face each other.

Even as it is
there are compensations
for having to meet
nose to neck
chest to scapula
groin to rump
when they sleep.

They look, at least,
as if they were going
in the same direction.

ADRIAN HENRI
WITHOUT YOU

Without you every morning would be like going back
 to work after a holiday,
Without you I couldn't stand the smell of the East
 Lancs Road,
Without you ghost ferries would cross the Mersey
 manned by skeleton crews,
Without you I'd probably feel happy and have more
 money and time and nothing to do with it,
Without you I'd have to leave my stillborn poems on
 other people's doorsteps, wrapped in brown paper,
Without you there'd never be sauce to put on sausage
 butties,
Without you plastic flowers in shop windows would just
 be plastic flowers in shop windows,
Without you I'd spend my summers picking morosely
 over the remains of train crashes,
Without you white birds would wrench themselves free
 from my paintings and fly off dripping blood into
 the night,
Without you green apples wouldn't taste greener,
Without you Mothers wouldn't let their children
 play out after tea,
Without you every musician in the world would forget
 how to play the blues,
Without you Public Houses would be public again,

Without you the Sunday Times colour supplement
    would come out in black-and-white,
Without you indifferent colonels would shrug their
    shoulders and press the button,
Without you they'd stop changing the flowers in
    Piccadilly Gardens,
Without you Clark Kent would forget how to become
    Superman,
Without you Sunshine Breakfast would only consist of
    Cornflakes,
Without you there'd be no colour in Magic colouring
    books,
Without you Mahler's 8th would only be performed by
    street musicians in derelict houses,
Without you they'd forget to put the salt in every
    packet of crisps,
Without you it would be an offence punishable by a fine
    of up to £200 or two months imprisonment to be
    found in possession of curry powder,
Without you riot police are massing in quiet
    side streets,
Without you all streets would be one way the other way,
Without you there'd be no one not to kiss goodnight
    when we quarrel,
Without you the first martian to land would turn round
    and go away again,
Without you they'd forget to change the weather,
Without you blind men would sell unlucky heather,

35

Without you there would be
no landscapes/no stations/no houses,
no chipshops/no quiet villages/no seagulls
on beaches/no hopscotch on pavements/no
night/no morning/ there'd be no city no country
Without you

HUGO WILLIAMS
THE COUPLE UPSTAIRS

Shoes instead of slippers down the stairs.
She ran out with her clothes

And the front door banged and I saw her
Walking crookedly, like naked, to a car.

She was not always with him up there,
And yet they seemed inviolate, like us,
Our loves in sympathy. Her going

Thrills and frightens us. We come awake
And talk excitedly about ourselves, like guests.

STANLEY J. SHARPLESS

IN PRAISE OF COCOA, CUPID'S NIGHTCAP

*[Lines written upon hearing the startling news
that cocoa is, in fact, a mild aphrodisiac]*

Half-past nine – high time for supper;
'Cocoa, love?' 'Of course, my dear.'
Helen thinks it quite delicious,
John prefers it now to beer.
Knocking back the sepia potion,
Hubby winks, says 'Who's for bed?'
'Shan't be long', says Helen softly,
Cheeks a faintly flushing red.
For they've stumbled on the secret
Of a love that never wanes,
Rapt beneath the tumbled bedclothes,
Cocoa coursing through their veins.

LOUIS MACNEICE
LES SYLPHIDES

Life in a day: he took his girl to the ballet;
Being shortsighted himself could hardly see it –
   The white skirts in the grey
   Glade and the swell of the music
   Lifting the white sails.

Calyx upon calyx, canterbury bells in the breeze
The flowers on the left mirror to the flowers on the right
   And the naked arms above
   The powdered faces moving
   Like seaweed in a pool.

Now, he thought, we are floating – ageless, oarless –
Now there is no separation, from now on
   You will be wearing white
   Satin and a red sash
   Under the waltzing trees.

But the music stopped, the dancers took their curtain,
The river had come to a lock – a shuffle of programmes –
   And we cannot continue down
   Stream unless we are ready
   To enter the lock and drop.

So they were married – to be the more together –
And found they were never again so much together,
   Divided by the morning tea,
   By the evening paper,
   By children and tradesmen's bills.

Waking at times in the night she found assurance
In his regular breathing but wondered whether
   It was really worth it and where
   The river had flowed away
   And where were the white flowers.

♥

LOUIS MACNEICE
FOR X

   When clerks and navvies fondle
      Beside canals their wenches,
   In rapture or in coma
      The haunches that they handle,
   And the orange moon sits idle
      Above the orchard slanted –
   Upon such easy evenings
      We take our loves for granted.

But when, as now, the creaking
    Trees on the hills of London
Like bison charge their neighbours
    In wind that keeps us waking
And in the draught the scalloped
    Lampshade swings a shadow,
We think of love bound over –
    The mortgage on the meadow.

And one lies lonely, haunted
    By limbs he half remembers,
And one, in wedlock, wonders
    Where is the girl he wanted;
And some sit smoking, flicking
    The ash away and feeling
For love gone up like vapour
    Between the floor and ceiling.

But now when winds are curling
    The trees do you come closer,
Close as an eyelid fasten
    My body in darkness, darling;
Switch the light off and let me
    Gather you up and gather
The power of trains advancing
    Further, advancing further.

TOM PAULIN
IN A NORTHERN LANDSCAPE

Ingela is thin and she never smiles,
The man is tall and wears the same subdued colours.
Their accents might be anywhere, both seem perfect
And spend only the winter months here.
They own a stone cottage at the end of a field
That slopes to rocks and a gunmetal sea.

Their silence is part of the silence at this season,
Is so wide that these solitaries seem hemmed in
By a distance of empty sea, a bleak mewing
Of gulls perched on their chimney, expecting storm.
They sit in basket chairs on their verandah,
Reading and hearing music from a tiny transistor.

Their isolation is almost visible:
Blue light on snow or sour milk in a cheese-cloth
Resembles their mysterious element.
They pickle herrings he catches, eat sauerkraut
And make love on cold concrete in the afternoons;
Eaters of yoghurt, they enjoy austere pleasures.

At night oil lamps burn in their small windows
And blocks of pressed peat glow in a simple fireplace.
Arc lamps on the new refinery at the point
Answer their lights; there is blackness and the sound of
                                                    surf.
They are so alike that they have no need to speak,
Like oppressed orphans who have won a fiery privacy.

41

PARTING ♥ ♥ ♥

YEHUDA AMICHAI
QUICK AND BITTER

The end was quick and bitter.
Slow and sweet was the time between us,
Slow and sweet were the nights
When my hands did not touch one another in despair
But with the love of your body
Which came between them.

And when I entered into you
It seemed then that great happiness
Could be measured with the precision
Of sharp pain. Quick and bitter.

Slow and sweet were the nights.
Now is as bitter and grinding as sand –
'We shall be sensible' and similar curses.

And as we stray further from love
We multiply the words,
Words and sentences long and orderly.
Had we remained together
We could have become a silence.

*Translated from the Hebrew by
Assia Gutmann*

GOODBYE

So we must say Goodbye, my darling,
And go, as lovers go, for ever;
Tonight remains, to pack and fix on labels
And make an end of lying down together.

I put a final shilling in the gas,
And watch you slip your dress below your knees
And lie so still I hear your rustling comb
Modulate the autumn in the trees.

And all the countless things I shall remember
Lay mummy-cloths of silence round my head;
I fill the carafe with a drink of water;
You say 'We paid a guinea for this bed,'

And then, 'We'll leave some gas, a little warmth
For the next resident, and these dry flowers,'
And turn your face away, afraid to speak
The big word, that Eternity is ours.

Your kisses close my eyes and yet you stare
As though God struck a child with nameless fears;
Perhaps the water glitters and discloses
Time's chalice and its limpid useless tears.

Everything we renounce except our selves;
Selfishness is the last of all to go;
Our sighs are exhalations of the earth,
Our footprints leave a track across the snow.

We made the universe to be our home,
Our nostrils took the wind to be our breath,
Our hearts are massive towers of delight,
We stride across the seven seas of death.

Yet when all's done you'll keep the emerald
I placed upon your finger in the street;
And I will keep the patches that you sewed
On my old battledress tonight, my sweet.

CHRISTINA ROSSETTI
REMEMBER

Remember me when I am gone away,
Gone far away into the silent land;
When you can no more hold me by the hand,
Nor I half turn to go yet turning stay.
Remember me when no more day by day
You tell me of our future that you plann'd:
Only remember me; you understand
It will be late to counsel then or pray.
Yet if you should forget me for a while
And afterwards remember, do not grieve:
For if the darkness and corruption leave
A vestige of the thoughts that once I had,
Better by far you should forget and smile
Than that you should remember and be sad.

♥ ♥ ♥

BRIAN PATTEN
SONG FOR LAST YEAR'S WIFE

Alice, this is my first winter
of waking without you, of knowing
that you, dressed in familiar clothes
are elsewhere, perhaps not even
conscious of our anniversary. Have
you noticed? The earth's still as hard,
the same empty gardens exist; it is
as if nothing special had changed.
I wake with another mouth feeding
from me, yet still feel as if
Love had not the right
to walk out of me. A year now. So
what? you say. I send out my spies
to discover what you are doing. They smile,
return, tell me your body's as firm,
you are as alive, as warm and inviting
as when I knew you first. . . . Perhaps it is
the winter, its isolation from other seasons,
that sends me your ghost to witness
when I wake. Somebody came here today, asked
how you were keeping, what
you were doing. I imagine you
waking in another city, touched
by this same hour. So ordinary
a thing as loss comes now and touches me.

LOUIS ZUKOFSKY
CATULLUS VIII

Miserable Catullus, stop being foolish
And admit it's over,
The sun shone on you those days
When your girl had you
When you gave it to her
          like nobody else ever will.
Everywhere together then, always at it
And you liked it and she can't say
                    she didn't

Yes, those days glowed.
Now she doesn't want it: why
          should you, washed out
Want to. Don't trail her,
Don't eat yourself up alive,
Show some spunk, stand up
                    and take it.
So long, girl. Catullus
          can take it.
He won't bother you, he won't
                    be bothered:
But you'll be, nights.

What do you want to live for?
Whom will you see?
Who'll say you're pretty?
Who'll give it to you now?
Whose name will you have?
Kiss what guy? bite whose

                    lips?

Come on Catullus, you can

                  take it.

ALEXANDER PUSHKIN

I loved you; even now I may confess,
   Some embers of my love their fire retain;
But do not let it cause you more distress,
   I do not want to sadden you again.
Hopeless and tonguetied, yet I loved you dearly
   With pangs the jealous and the timid know;
So tenderly I loved you, so sincerely,
   I pray God grant another love you so.

Translated from the Russian by
Reginald Mainwaring Hewitt

W. H. AUDEN
'STOP ALL THE CLOCKS, CUT OFF THE TELEPHONE'

Stop all the clocks, cut off the telephone,
Prevent the dog from barking with a juicy bone,
Silence the pianos and with muffled drum
Bring out the coffin, let the mourners come.

Let aeroplanes circle moaning overhead
Scribbling on the sky the message He Is Dead,
Put the crêpe bows round the white necks of the
                                        public doves,
Let the traffic policemen wear black cotton gloves.

He was my North, my South, my East and West,
My working week and my Sundays rest,
My noon, my midnight, my talk, my song;
I thought that love would last for ever: I was wrong.

The stars are not wanted now: put out every one;
Pack up the moon and dismantle the sun;
Pour away the ocean and sweep up the wood.
For nothing now can ever come to any good.

WHO?

Who can I
spend my life
with
Who can I
listen to Georges Brassens
singing
'Les amoureux des bancs publiques'
with
Who can I
go to Paris with
getting drunk at night with
tall welldressed spades
Who can I
quarrel with
outside chipshops
in sidestreets
on landings
Who else
can sing along with Shostakovitch
Who else
would sign a Christmas card
'Cannonball'
Who else
can work the bathroom geyser

Who else
drinks as much bitter
Who else
makes all my favourite meals
except the ones I make
myself
Who else
Would bark back at dogs
in the moonlit lamplight streets
Who else
would I find
waiting dark bigeyed
in a corner of a provincial jazzclub
You say
we don't get on
anymore
but
who can I
laugh on beaches with
wondering at the noise
the limpets make
still sucking in the tide
Who
can I
buy
my next Miles Davis record
to share with

who
makes coffee the way I like it
and
love the way I used to like it
who
came in from the sun
the day
the world went spinning away
from me
who
doesn't wash the clothes I always want
who
spends my money
who
wears my dressing gown
and always leaves the sleeves turned up
who
makes me feel
as empty as the house does
when she's not there
who
else
but
you

for Joyce

CECIL DAY LEWIS
THE ALBUM

I see you, a child
In a garden sheltered for buds and playtime,
Listening as if beguiled
By a fancy beyond your years and the flowering maytime.
The print is faded: soon there will be
No trace of that pose enthralling,
Nor visible echo of my voice distantly calling
'Wait! Wait for me!'

Then I turn the page
To a girl who stands like a questioning iris
By the waterside, at an age
That asks every mirror to tell what the heart's desire is.
The answer she finds in that oracle stream
Only time could affirm or disprove,
Yet I wish I was there to venture a warning, 'Love
Is not what you dream'.

Next you appear
As if garlands of wild felicity crowned you –
Courted, caressed, you wear
Like immortelles the lovers and friends around you.
'They will not last you, rain or shine,
They are but straws and shadows,'
I cry: 'Give not to those charming desperadoes
What was made to be mine.'

One picture is missing –
The last. It would show me a tree stripped bare
By intemperate gales, her amazing
Noonday of blossom spoilt which promised so fair.
Yet, scanning those scenes at your heyday taken,
I tremble, as one who must view
In the crystal a doom he could never deflect – yes, I too
Am fruitlessly shaken.

I close the book;
But the past slides out of its leaves to haunt me
And it seems, wherever I look,
Phantoms of irreclaimable happiness taunt me.
Then I see her, petalled in new-blown hours,
Beside me – 'All you love most there
Has blossomed again,' she murmurs, 'all that
                         you missed there
Has grown to be yours.'

♥ ♥ ♥

EDWARD THOMAS
NO ONE SO MUCH AS YOU

No one so much as you
Loves this my clay,
Or would lament as you
Its dying day.

You know me through and through
Though I have not told,
And though with what you know
You are not bold.

None ever was so fair
As I thought you:
Not a word can I bear
Spoken against you.

All that I ever did
For you seemed coarse
Compared with what I hid
Nor put in force.

My eyes scarce dare meet you
Lest they should prove
I but respond to you
And do not love.

We look and understand,
We cannot speak –
Except in trifles and
Words the most weak.

For I at most accept
Your love, regretting
That is all: I have kept
Only a fretting

That I could not return
All that you gave
And could not ever burn
With the love you have,

Till sometimes it did seem
Better it were
Never to see you more
Than linger here

With only gratitude
Instead of love –
A pine in solitude
Cradling a dove.

♥ ♥ ♥

ROBERT GRAVES
CALL IT A GOOD MARRIAGE

Call it a good marriage –
For no one ever questioned
Her warmth, his masculinity,
Their interlocking views;
Except one stray graphologist
Who frowned in speculation
At her h's and her s's,
His p's and w's.

Though few would still subscribe
To the monogamic axiom
That strife below the hip-bones
Need not estrange the heart,
Call it a good marriage:
More drew these two together,
Despite a lack of children,
Than pulled them apart.

Call it a good marriage.
They never fought in public,
They acted circumspectly
And faced the world with pride;
Thus the hazards of their love-bed
Were none of our damned business –
Till as juryman we sat on
Two deaths by suicide.

MICHAEL DRAYTON
'SINCE THERE'S NO HELP,
COME, LET US KISS AND PART'

Since there's no help, come, let us kiss and part –
Nay, I have done: you get no more of me;
And I am glad, yea, glad with all my heart
That thus so cleanly I myself can free.
Shake hands forever, cancel all our vows,
And when we meet at any time again,
Be it not seen in either of our brows
That we one jot of former love retain.
Now at the last gasp of love's latest breath,
When, his pulse failing, Passion speechless lies,
When Faith is kneeling by his bed of death,
And innocence is closing up his eyes, –
Now, if thou wouldst, when all have given him over,
From death to life thou mightst him yet recover.

INDEX

ANON
Plucking the rushes 9

YEHUDA AMICHAI (1924–)
We did it 26
Quick and Bitter 45

PETRONIUS ARBITER (1st cent. AD)
'Good God, what a night that was' 25

W. H. AUDEN (1907–73)
'Stop all the clocks, cut off the telephone' 52

HILAIRE BELLOC (1870–1953)
Juliet 11

JOHN BERRYMAN (1914–)
'Filling her compact & delicious body' 14

SIR JOHN BETJEMAN (1906–)
A Subaltern's Love-Song 12

RUPERT BROOKE (1887–1915)
The Hill 8

C. P. CAVAFY (1863–1933)
To Remain 24

E. E. CUMMINGS (1894–1962)
'i like my body when it is with your' 22

MICHAEL DRAYTON (1563–1631)
'Since there's no help, come, let us kiss and part' 61

DOUGLAS DUNN (1942–)
Modern Love 31

ROBERT GRAVES (1895–)
Symptoms of love 16
'Call it a good marriage' 60

ADRIAN HENRI (1932–)
Without You 34
Who? 53

D. H. LAWRENCE (1885–1930)
Gloire de Dijon 15
New Year's Eve 21

ALUN LEWIS
Goodbye 46

CECIL DAY LEWIS (1904–72)
The Album 56

LOUIS MACNEICE (1907–63)
Les Sylphides 38
For X 39

DOROTHY PARKER (1893–1967)
One Perfect Rose 17

BRIAN PATTEN (1946–)
Party Piece 23
Song for Last Year's Wife 49

TOM PAULIN (1949–)
In a Northern Landscape 41

ALEXANDER PUSHKIN (1799–1837)
'I loved you; even now I may confess' 51

ISAAC ROSENBERG (1890–1918)
You and I 10

CHRISTINA ROSSETTI (1830–94)
The First Day 7
Remember 48

STANLEY J. SHARPLESS
In praise of cocoa, cupid's nightcap 37

STEPHEN SPENDER (1909–)
Daybreak 27

ANNE STEVENSON (1933–)
The Marriage 33

EDWARD THOMAS (1878–1917)
'No one so much as you' 58

HUGO WILLIAMS (1942–)
Tides 32
The Couple Upstairs 36

LOUIS ZUKOFSKY (1904–78)
Catallus VIII 50

ACKNOWLEDGEMENTS

For permission to reprint copyright material, the publishers gratefully acknowledge the following:

Harper and Row Inc. for poems by Yehuda Amichai; Faber and Faber and Random House for the poem by W. H. Auden; A. D. Peters for 'Juliet' by Hilaire Belloc; Farrer, Strauss Geroux for the poem by John Berryman; John Murray for the poem by Sir John Betjeman; The Hogarth Press and Harcourt Brace for the poem by C. P. Cavafy; William Collins Ltd, and Liverwright Publishing Corp. for the poem by E. E. Cummings; Faber and Faber for the poem by Douglas Dunn; A. P. Watt for the poems by Robert Graves; Deborah Rogers for the poems by Adrian Henri; Lawrence Pollinger for the poems by D. H. Lawrence; Allen and Unwin for the poem by Alun Lewis; Jonathan Cape for the poem by Cecil Day Lewis; Faber and Faber for poems by Louis MacNeice; Duckworth Ltd. for the poem by Dorothy Parker; Allen and Unwin for the poems by Brian Patten; Faber and Faber for the poem by Tom Paulin; The University of Michigan Press for the poem by Petronius Arbiter; Basil Blackwell for the poem by Alexander Pushkin; Chatto and Windus for the poem by Isaac Rosenberg; *The New Statesman* for the poem by Stanley J. Sharpless; Faber and Faber and Random House for the poem by Stephen Spender; Oxford University Press for the poems by Anne Stevenson and Hugo Williams; Jonathan Cape for the poem by Louis Zukofsky; Constable Publications and Alfred Knopf for 'Plucking the Rushes' translated by Arthur Waley.